John Luttrell's

I Saw the Elephant

John Luttrell's

I Saw the Elephant

by

Betty Luttrell and Laquata Potts

DORRANCE PUBLISHING CO., INC.
PITTSBURGH, PENNSYLVANIA 15222

ISBN # 0-8059-5880-0
Printed in the United States of America

First Printing

For information or to order additional books, please write:
Dorrance Publishing Co., Inc.
701 Smithfield Street
Third Floor
Pittsburgh, Pennsylvania 15222
U.S.A.
1-800-788-7654
Or visit our web site and on-line catalog at *www.dorrancepublishing.com*

This book is dedicated to John Luttrell's children and grandchildren.

Date	Action
June 25, 1950	North Korea invades South Korea; ignores UN demand that the Communists stop fighting and retreat to 38th parallel
June 27, 1950	President Truman orders U.S. air and naval forces to South Korea. UN asks its members to aid South Korea
June 30, 1950	Truman orders ground forces into action
July 5, 1950	American troops first meet North Koreans at Osan
September 8, 1950	Allied troops stop the Communist advance at the Pusan Perimeter
September 15, 1950	Allied troops land at Inchon
September 26, 1950	UN forces under General MacArthur capture Seoul
October 19, 1950	Allies capture Pyongyang, North Korean capital
October 25, 1950	China enters war. U.S. and Chinese troops meet at Changjin Reservoir and at Onjong. The Chinese withdraw on Nov. 6
November 26–27, 1950	Chinese attack Allies and force an extended retreat
January 16, 1951	Allies move north and reoccupy Seoul on March 14
April 11, 1951	Truman removes MacArthur from command
July 10, 1951	Truce talks begin, but fighting continues
April 28, 1952	Communist negotiators refuse to allow voluntary repatriation of prisoners
October 8, 1952	Truce talks are broken off
March 28, 1953	UN proposes an exchange of sick and wounded prisoners; Communists accept
April 26, 1953	Truce talks resume
July 27, 1953	Armistice agreement signed. Fighting stops
1954	Attempts to establish a permanent peace plan fail

CHINA

Chongjin • RUSSIA

Yalu River

• Chosan ▲ Changjin Reservoir

NORTH KOREA

Sinuiju

Hamhung •

Korea Bay • Hungnam

★ Pyongyang • Wonsan
▲

Sea of Japan

Taebaek Mtns.

Nampo

Heartbreak Ridge —— Armistice Line

Panmunjom ▲ Punchbowl
Kaesong

38th Parallel — — —

★ Seoul Chuncheon

Inchon — ▲
Wolmi-do • Wonju

Yellow Sea ▲ Osan Taebaek

Chongju • SOUTH

Taejon • Yechon KOREA

▲ Battles Naktong River

Chonju • Taegu

0   100 Miles
0   100 Kilometers

Chinju Masan

Kwangju Pusan

Mokpo

JAPAN •

Preface

My military career lasted twenty-five years. It spanned three wars: World War II, the Korean War, and the beginning of the Vietnam War. I saw combat action in World War II and Korea and spent thirty-three months in a prisoner of war camp.

Every day I remember the battles I was in that brought near-death experiences. I fought to survive and to come home. The survival techniques that I learned from experiences and the techniques I learned listening to soldiers' stories helped me through overpowering situations.

My book is titled *I Saw the Elephant*. "I saw the elephant" is a statement that was introduced during the Civil War. It means to see life or to gain experience during overwhelming odds. "Under overwhelming odds" are the key words I'll use to explain my survival in three major incidents.

I saw the elephant when I trained my gun on a Japanese submarine that was trying to kill men on a cargo ship. The Japanese submarine outgunned the cargo ship.

I saw the elephant when I was trying to bring down a kamikaze. I saw him slump over his wheel and die in just a few blinks of the eye as he veered off his path of my destruction.

I saw the elephant while fighting hordes of Chinese soldiers. I fought against their machine gunners, their snipers, their tanks, and their grenades and came out with a minor wound.

This is my story that I spoke into a tape recorder. My wife, Betty Luttrell, and her sister, Luquata Potts, co-authored the actual interpretation and writing of this book. There were many long hours put into this project; therefore, I wish to express my thanks to these two ladies.

There were other family members and friends who helped make this story possible. I am grateful to my son, Anthony Luttrell, for the inspiration he gave me, as well as the support with my memoirs. I am grateful to Tim and Teresa Stump in helping to type the first draft of this book. I also wish to thank Tony Jones for his support in helping to gather pertinent material.

Figure A. Purple Heart for combat duty.
Figure B. A spoon that John fashioned in Camp 5.

Chapter 1

I was born in a log cabin in a mining camp called Disney located in the Appalachian Mountains of Kentucky. I grew up surrounded by my dad, mom, eight brothers, and two pretty brown-eyed sisters. I was the number five son in this melee of family unity.

The seasons in the mountains that surrounded us gave us beauty from dogwood blossoms in spring covering the hillside to emerald green and chartreuse in summer. Gold, red, and brown ushered autumn in. The winters went from stark barren tree trunks to a wonderland of snow-covered mountains.

My life with my parents and siblings was happy. We were poor in a monetary sense, but the mountains provided us with berries, grapes, game, and all things of wonder to stir the imagination of a small boy.

My parents taught a code of honor that gave us a sense of well being and the confidence to do whatever we had to do in the tests of life. We were taught to help our fellow man and not to ask anything in return. This code gave us a sense of individuality, independence, and responsibility.

My formal school years consisted of grades one through six. I was taught reading, writing, and arithmetic. At about age fifteen, with the permission of my parents, I spent one year in the Civilian Conservation Corp. I helped build an enclosure for the testing of poisonous gasses at Twilla, Utah. My life as a young man had begun.

Chapter II

In 1943 I enlisted in the Navy in my hometown of Harlan, Kentucky. World War II was in full swing. I went to boot camp in the Great Lakes Station at Great Lakes, Illinois. After boot camp, basic training included rifle and later jujitsu training. I turned into a fighting machine.

From boot camp, I went to gunnery training in Gulf Port, Mississippi. In gunnery training, I learned about the weapons that were to be used on board the *Liberty* ship. This ship carried three-inch antiaircraft guns and fifty-millimeter antiaircraft weapons, and four-inch cannons were carried on the stern of the ship.

Germany had been kicking up a fuss in the Atlantic, damaging and destroying our ships. New recruits who had just come out of basic training were labeled by the military as "shark bait."

We were the Navy Armed Guards—nicknamed "shark bait"—assigned to a civilian merchant marine ship. We wore regular army uniforms, worked for the army, and were paid by the army, but we belonged to the navy. Our job was to protect merchant marine ships because we were highly trained gunners and we guarded war supplies that our ship was carrying to and from Australia. We needed relief gunners, so we trained the seamen who worked on the ship.

After Gulf Port, Mississippi, I was shipped to Treasure Island, California, near San Francisco. There we continued our intense training in self-defense. We learned to recognize aircraft and different ships both friend and foe. We had twenty days shore leave and then we trained for sea duty.

Chapter III

From Treasure Island, I was assigned to the steamship *Juan Pueblo Duarte*. When we boarded the ship, we were told our Swedish Captain believed we were too young to protect his ship. Our gunnery officer said to the captain, "Have your carpenter secure some oil drums on a raft and turn it loose. I'll show you what my men can do."

The barrels drifted the distance of about a mile out. Standing at the four-inch cannon at the rear of the ship, I was told to fire at the oil drums. I fired one round over the target and one round under. Then I made a direct hit and sunk the raft and barrels. The captain came back and told our crew he would never call us kids again and that he would go anywhere with us as his protectors.

We set sail at a snail's pace from San Francisco. Staying out of harm's way, we wandered around the Northern Pacific and then headed for Townsville, Australia. We traveled for thirty days.

Most of my fellow armed guards, as well as my gunnery captain, had never been to sea. One day, during a rest period, I was sitting on the fantail at the rear end of the ship reading a book. My gunnery captain asked me what I was reading. I said, "I'm reading a Zane Grey book."

Then he said, "What do you think of this ocean and the long time we have been at open sea?"

I said, "Sir, I think this is the biggest damn creek I ever saw."

Chapter IV

We arrived in Townsville, Australia, where we unloaded our cargo and headed for Brisbane, Australia, to pick up new cargo and troops. We then headed for the New Guinea coast, transporting the Forty-first Infantry Division to New Guinea. We traveled back and forth from New Guinea to Australia for eleven months, transporting the Forty-first Infantry, who were fighting the Japanese along the coast of New Guinea and who were slowly taking the island back from Japan.

One morning we left Brisbane, Australia, heading toward New Guinea. We were transporting weapons, Australians nicknamed Aussies, and soldiers from the Forty-first Infantry. We came upon a cargo ship being assaulted by a submarine. The cargo ship was outgunned by the submarine. The radioman on the cargo ship radioed us asking for our help. The cargo ship was like a sitting duck waiting to be shot. The submarine was too far away for the cargo ship to reach with their guns, but the submarine kept shooting at and hitting the cargo ship. Our guns were heavier guns than the cargo ship's. We manned five-inch thirty-eight millimeter guns that could reach out at least six miles. We knew if we could get the submarine to dive that we could outrun it. The submarine could only travel at eight knots a mile, and we could travel at least twelve to fourteen knots. I aimed my gun and shot over the submarine. I aimed again and shot under the submarine. I aimed the third time and the sub dived. The men on the cargo ship jumped up and down and shouted with happiness; they were safe once more. This is the first time I saw the elephant.

When we sailed into Hollanda, New Guinea, Eleanor Roosevelt was visiting with the troops, and we came ashore to listen to what she had to say. We were all dressed in our khaki uniforms with just a Navy hat, and she asked the master of ceremony who we were. He said we were the armed guard troops. She said, "Oh! The orphans of the Navy."

The Forty-first Division, in conjunction with the Australians, took New Guinea back from Japan, but there were straggling Japanese soldiers in caves and in the bush. The Australian soldiers were in charge of the New Guinea natives, who were fierce warriors, and the Japanese soldiers were afraid of them. The Aussies put a bounty on the heads of any Japanese soldier killed. They exchanged food, clothing, and other items for the ears extracted from dead Japanese soldiers.

The New Guinea natives were surprisingly honest. For example, one day I observed natives walking on shore by a pile of old clothing and rags discarded from our ship. They asked us in sign language if they could have the old clothes, and we replied in sign language that they could. Their faces lit up with smiles, and we were awed at their honesty and integrity.

Off the northern coastline of New Guinea, on an isolated island called Biak, we spotted what we thought was a log across the road. But this log turned out to be a monstrous snake about twenty feet in length.

After the tour of about eleven months transporting troops along the New Guinea coastlines, we picked up troops of the Forty-first Division and Australian soldiers on their way home for shore leave. Men from the Forty-first Division entertained us with stories about their fighting tactics that gave us clues to what real battles were all about. After we left Australia, we headed back to Treasure Island in California and were given shore leave and told we would be reassigned to another ship.

Chapter V

The ship, *John Owen*, was the next ship I was assigned to. We headed with troops of the Forty-first Division toward the Philippines and picked up the escort, *Man of War*, because we were carrying bombs, torpedoes, and other war supplies.

As we were heading for the Leyte Gulf in the Philippines, Admiral William Hallsey, commander of the Pacific Fleet, was giving the Japanese Fleet hell. Our escort ship and all the other cruisers in the area headed toward the Gulf ready to fight in this battle.

The Japanese thought they had suckered the United States fleet into the Gulf to trap them, but Admiral William "Bull" Hallsey outsmarted them and did immense damage to the Japanese fleet. The crippled Japanese fleet limped back out into the Pacific Ocean and into oblivion. Admiral Bull Hallsey went down in the history books as a good leader and an excellent tactician.

Meanwhile, our ship floated along with several other ships until morning. About a hundred miles out of the Leyte Gulf, we cut our engines along with other cargo ships. Around midnight of the same day, we received orders to proceed ahead to the Leyte Gulf. We traveled at a pace of about fourteen knots and arrived at our destination around daybreak the next morning.

Chapter VI

Arriving in the Leyte Gulf, the sea battle had already been fought, and our ships, destroyers, cruisers, and torpedo boats were showing the awful rigors of war. Some ships had burns and holes in the sides so big that a truck could be driven through them. I do not believe that there were battleships in this battle, but there were a great number of cruisers. These ships were smaller than a battleship but had a large amount of firepower.

We dropped anchor and went ashore to visit old friends from the Forty-first Division. There was utter devastation around us. On the docks, hundreds of dead sailors were being stacked one on top of the other like cordwood.

While waiting to unload our war supplies, my sailor friends and I were playing cards and listening to Tokyo Rose, the Japanese Army's queen of propaganda. We wanted to listen to her broadcast because sometimes she would give us warnings of what was about to happen, and she also would play the current music of the forties. We laughed at her when she told us that we would never see our girlfriends and families again. While listening and laughing at Tokyo Rose, my buddies and I spied Japanese Zeros coming from the North over the mountains for a follow-up attack. Since the fighting ships had already moved out, the battle would be between our merchant ships and Japanese Zero war planes.

We ran to our guns and waited for them to attack. The zeros came in low enough to make a torpedo run. This action hampered our firing power, because we were afraid we would hit our own ships. After the battle, the captain of a damaged merchant ship, in a moment of humor, raised a white bed sheet on his flagpole. When he was asked why the white surrender flag, he replied, "I cannot whip the Japanese Navy and the American Navy at the same time. So I surrender!" This battle lasted for approximately fifteen minutes, and there was not much damage to our merchant ships. After a couple of days, we set sail along with our escorts out of the gulf, heading toward Treasure Island, California.

Chapter VII

Leaving California, our protector, the warship *New Mexico*, and our steamships loaded with war supplies docked in Nagasaki Bay, Okinawa. While planning the invasion of Japan, Tokyo Rose warned us about kamikaze planes being manned by young and old pilots. These pilots were on suicide missions and would try to dive their planes into our ships. Tokyo Rose told us that these planes were armed with poison gas and that this poison gas would kill all of us in the bay. We manned our weapons and took along with us our gas masks.

Before the kamikaze planes came into the bay, Admiral Nimitz met the kamikazes in the first line of defense and shot down a good portion of the planes. About twenty to twenty-five planes squeezed through the first line of defense. Then our U.S. Air Force stationed in Okinawa flew out to meet the remaining planes. Several destroyers met with death when diving planes turned the destroyers into balls of fire.

One kamikaze broke through and headed toward our merchant ships. He surveyed a couple of ships and then came toward us. I suppose he could see the bombs, torpedoes, and five thousand jugs of chemicals sitting on our deck. The kamikaze circled our ship and dove toward us. We were at our weapons ready to shoot. I manned a twenty-millimeter cannon on the bridge. All the weapons from our ship and other ships around us were firing at the kamikaze. I was strapped into a shoulder and hand harness. I stood with my weapon all the way back, firing with all the fury I could muster. This was the second time I saw the elephant.

The plane came so close to me that I could see the pilot. I saw him get hit and slump over to one side. I'm not sure who killed him—someone else or me. The plane veered off to the right and hit the water about seventy yards from our ship. When the plane hit the water and went down into the sea, we were surprised that the plane didn't explode.

This air battle lasted about an hour, and when it was finished, we breathed a sigh of relief. Fear had hit my body so hard that within the next ten days I turned completely gray around the edges of my hair, and later the gray hair fell out.

We left Nagasaki Bay and went to Fort Himaume, California, where we all—including all the sailors on board the Henry Durrant—received a commendation. The commendation was issued to our gunnery officer, and he commended us for bravery under extreme battle conditions. Because we had shot down a kamikaze, a flag with the rising sun was painted on the smokestack of our merchant ship.

For the next several days, we were treated like heroes. The Merchant Marines took up a collection among themselves to finance shore leave for us. In all the bars we went into, we were provided with free drinks. Because I was not yet twenty-one, I could not legally buy an alcoholic drink. However, the bartenders figured if I could go into battle for my country, I was entitled to a drink. This was a delight to me, a weary soldier.

The war was over in Europe! After the final assault in Nagasaki Bay, we were glad that President Truman halted our plans for the invasion of Japan. If he hadn't done that, we would have had to go in and kill every soldier in Japan. President Truman brought an end to the war with Japan when he ordered the atomic bomb dropped on Hiroshima and Nagasaki.

Chapter VIII

I was on a point system for the duration of the war plus six months more. So I went back to sea to sweep for mines in a vessel YMS number 338, which we operated out of Shanghai and Hong Kong. In our ship made of wood, we gathered mines that had been planted by the Japanese along the West Coast of Korea to the East Coast of Indochina, now known as Vietnam. The Japanese had supposedly cleared this area, but we found that there were mines still hiding in these waters. The mines were attached to the bottom of the bay, so we would use our pig-out to cut them loose to float to the top of the water; then we exploded them by shooting them with our cannons and guns.

While we were doing this work, I was a boson third-class petty officer. That meant that I took orders from the captain; when the captain left the boat, I was in charge.

My commander's name was Conrad Hilton. He came down on deck one day and asked me, "Do you know what that land mass is?"

I said, "No, sir, I do not."

He replied, "That is Korea. That will be where the next war will be fought."

From that day forward, I became interested and did a lot of research in world history and politics. Later I found that this research aided me in my military career.

We swept the coast of Indochina, were I learned how to use depth charges. When we had free time, we would spend a few days on the beaches of Indochina before we took our new assignments.

One day, while playing on the beach, we met Vietnamese natives who were fishermen. These fishermen were old men, and my buddies and I communicated with them by using hand signals. We left the fishermen and went back aboard our ship to get our new assignments. Into the bay came a French cruiser, firing on the civilians and noncombatants on the beach. This action disgusted us, and our radioman called them and asked, "What the hell is going on?"

A crisp voice came back across the radio stating, "This is our war, Yanks, stay out of it."

The incident was part of the beginning of the Vietnam War.

We went to Hong King, but our superiors sent us back out to sweep for mines. While on our search for mines one day, I was standing in the wheelhouse when my helmsman, who was also the lookout man, yelled, "Fish nets dead ahead." Since it was my watch and my responsibility, I took the wheel, picked up the tube to the engine room, and gave the engine crew orders what to do to get through the nets. I yelled, "Full speed ahead," and then, "Stop," until we maneuvered our boat through the nets. The ship was going crazy. The commander came to the bridge and wanted to know what in the hell I was doing. When I told him, he asked where I had learned to steer a ship. I replied, "Here, right here, sir." He complimented me and said, "If you had wound those nets around the screw of the propeller, you would be diving to get the nets off the propeller."

I said, "No problem, sir."

We sailed into uncharted territory sweeping for mines. We searched for mines, but we had not found any on that day. The pig, an object that looked like a barrel with a pointed nose, and the pig-out, the cutter that was attached to the pig by a wire, located new mines and cut them away from the bay. We decided that this area was clean, so I started pulling the mine gear back aboard the ship. About fifty yards out into the ocean, we spotted something in the water. When the cutter started pulling, we knew for sure that it was a mine. I stopped the winch that wound the cutter. I immediately called the bridge and yelled, "Who was the dumb son of a bitch who ordered full speed ahead?"

The commander yelled back, "I gave that order."

I very meekly replied, "Very well, sir."

Again we went full speed ahead. When the turbulence hit the mine, it exploded and sent water all over the deck. I had to tackle a couple of the men to get them to hit the deck. After all the excitement, we managed to get our gear back aboard and then head back to our main seaport. We rested up for our next venture.

Because mine sweeping was a high stress job and very dangerous, we were only out for three days and back into port for a two-day rest. Our ship was made out of wood, so dragging for mines and sailing through the water was very dangerous.

After the incident of the mine and before we left for our main port, our commander, Conrad Hilton, came to me and asked, "Boats, did that mine do damage to our ship?"

I replied, "Yes, sir, I rigged a boson chair and have already inspected the hull. We don't have holes all the way through, but enough of the wood

12

has been chipped away that it could weaken the hull. I think we will make it back to port."

The commander then said to me, "Boats, what kind of report should I give of this incident?"

I said, "An honest report, sir. If the commander of the fleet learns that you gave anything but an honest report, it's too bad in your case since you are an officer, sir."

He said, "I would never give anything other than an honest report."

Again, I rigged a boson chair by attaching lines to the chair. Its purpose was to hold a sailor while he worked on or examined the side of a ship. The sailor could maneuver himself up and down by a pulley attached to the chair. The commander commented that he had never rigged a chair, which led me to believe that I'd had more sea duty than he'd had.

The commander wanted to inspect the damage to the boat. I helped him into the boson chair. He lowered himself over the side, and when he had finished inspecting the side of the boat, I told him that I would send a man with paint and a paint bucket to paint the damaged part of the hull. Afterwards, we sailed into Hong Kong and made necessary repairs.

My duration of six months was over for me, so I headed back to the States. I boarded a transport ship out of Hong Kong. The ship moved north to Ten Sen, China, where we picked up ten thousand marines. They had been training Chaing Kai Shek's army until Mao Zedong had pushed Chaing Kai Shek's army into retreat and the marines had to evacuate. The marines told me the political views of both sides. The marines nicknamed Mao Zedong, "old mossy tongue." What I heard that day helped prepare me for the experiences I was to encounter in Korea.

On April 28, 1946, I was honorably discharged from the Navy and returned to the United States.

Chapter IX

After coming home to Kentucky, I tried to work in a coal mine; after awhile, I decided that was not for me. I then went to Michigan and got a job in an automobile factory and decided again that this was not what I wanted to do, so I went back to Kentucky.

One day I was in the county seat of Harlan, Kentucky. An ex-sailor and I were standing around talking about our navy days when a young man approached us and told us he wanted to join the army but could not pass the written exam. The ex-sailor, the young man, and I talked to the recruiting officer and told him if he would pass the young man, we would join up too. We informed him that all three of us would fill his much-needed quota. The recruiting officer said, "We are not having this conversation."

The ex-sailor and I sat on each side of the young man and helped him answer the true and false questions. The young man actually knew a few more answers than we did. Happily, we all passed the exam. The young man and I were assigned to the 101st Airborne Division non-jump status-training unit at Breckenridge, Kentucky.

We arrived at Breckenridge, where we began our basic training. Because there was a shortage of men in the military at that time, the army wanted all the experienced men they could get.

The field sergeant had five stripes on his shoulder. (If I'd still been in the Navy, I would have had equal rank.) One morning the field sergeant called all the ex-soldiers out in front of the group and assigned us to positions he wanted us to have. When he came to me, he gave me the job of acting platoon sergeant. The sergeant told me that the army needed all my experience to help train these young troops. I said, "No sweat, Sergeant. I can do that."

About a week later, the company commander called me into his office. He said that a lot of the ex-soldiers had higher ratings than me and had applied in writing for their ratings. He asked me if I wanted to apply for my rating. At that time, I considered myself just loafing in the military, so I told my commander no. I said I would train his troops, but I was not asking for rank. I said, "If after you see my work you think I'm worth it, then you can change my rating." I told him it did not bother me one bit to have other ex-sailor personnel in the company. Some of these ex-sailors were administrative-type yeoman and radar specialists. I didn't care that some of these ex-sailors had more rank than me.

I took these young recruits through basic training, and some of these youngsters in the platoon were a bunch of tough heads. They thought they could run the army and the rest of us would sit back and laugh at them.

Being in charge, I treated these soldiers as if I was a sergeant first class equal to a field first grade. The information that I gave them was good military thinking. I was trying to get an esprit de corps in this. I tried to show them that rank has its privileges and that rank had more responsibility than the experienced soldier.

The young man who enlisted at the same time I did was assigned to my division, but he wasn't in my platoon. I would see him occasionally and talk to him. This young man was not educated but wanted to stay in the army in the worst way. He came to me for advice when he could not handle the pressure his sergeant was putting on him. The sergeant noticed my relationship with this young man, and one day he came over to ask if the young man had anything on me. I told him the story of how the ex-sailor and myself had helped him get into the army. I told his platoon sergeant that the young man wanted to be a good soldier. I said, "You can put your money on the fact that he will try his best to be a good soldier." Finally, the platoon sergeant understood. The young man never came back to me for advice again. The platoon sergeant spent more time with him, and the young man graduated basic training with honors.

The field first sergeant was always kidding with me in a sarcastic way. He would say things like, "Swab wants to be a doughboy." I made up my mind not to let him get the best of me.

The field first informed me that my platoon was going to hike twenty-three miles. He said that when we returned he would have a blister inspection. All the men who went on the hike, including me, would have to take off their shoes for the field first to inspect our feet.

The announcement gave me time to figure out how to outsmart the field first. I got together with my platoon and told them that we were going on a twenty-three-mile hike and that the field first expected to see blisters on our feet when we returned. I told each man to stash extra socks under his clothes. I told them that we would hike for two hours and rest for ten minutes. "At each rest stop," I told them, "Put on your clean, dry socks, because wet socks cause your feet to blister when you are hiking."

When we returned, the field first sergeant came to inspect our feet. The sergeant said, "I don't understand this; there are no blisters. How did you accomplish this?" I let him know exactly what we had done. He congratulated me on this action. I think the field first learned something that day.

Chapter X

On the day I graduated from basic training, I applied for training school. I signed up for an enlisted correctional custody course. This course trained soldiers to guard military prisoners. I went to Fort Lee, Virginia, to begin enrollment in the course. The course was four weeks long. We trained in jujitsu, judo, and weapons. I'd had all this training during the war, so the class was a breeze to get through. Also, this training gave me another forty more hours in the arts.

From the correctional custody course, I learned that prisoners have a lot of time to plan how they are going to escape but that their guard only had a split second to make up his mind what he is going to do to prevent the man from escaping. This mind-set was the reason prisoners were chained while being transported. Also, this was why, at one time, the prison system had chain gangs. We were taught to never take a chance on a prisoner—good or bad. From Fort Lee, Virginia, I traveled to Fort Belvoir, Virginia, to enroll in a class on combat engineer construction. I stayed there four weeks and was then transferred to Fort Lewis, Washington. I was assigned to the Second Engineer Regiment of the Second Infantry Division. Later that division was ordered to go to Korea.

Chapter XI

The year was 1950, and Harry S. Truman was president. He warned North Korea not to cross the thirty-eighth parallel, but the North Koreans, with the aid of China and training from Russia, kept pushing south. The Second Division was fighting twenty miles from Pusan. They were fighting to hold this port, and North Korea was trying to kick them into the sea, but they held their ground.

At this time I was still at Fort Lewis, Washington, in charge of all weapons for my company. I was a corporal with a Beetle Bailey attitude. Since I had extensive knowledge in weapons from World War II, the company commander asked me if I would teach his non-commissioned officers transition firing. I told the company commander that to do this job it must be understood that if any of the non-coms got out of line or mouthed off, he would have to report directly to the company commander. I did not have to contend with bad behavior while I was teaching this course. Since transition firing is used when fighting door to door and it is tricky trying to decide who is the civilian and who is the enemy, instant decisions could be a matter of life and death. So I needed complete control over my group.

As always, there is usually one non-com who wants to sound off, and of course I got one who thought he was tough. I sent him to the company commander, who told me later that he took care of the problem.

The MOS evaluation board at Fort Lewis, Washington, was evaluating soldiers on their qualifications regardless of rank. After evaluating me, they wanted me to become a rigger or something similar in a smaller grade status. I let the board know that I would work in whatever capacity they wanted me to work, but I told the MOS board emphatically that I did not want to give up my combat foreman status. I had worked too hard and had taken many classes to achieve the status of construction foreman. I was assigned to a kitchen truck and worked out of a motor pool. About this time, we received alert orders that we would be leaving for Korea. All passes and leave were cancelled.

When I learned that all passes were cancelled, I felt really challenged. I went to the orderly room, looked around, and then began to blink my eyes, trying to work up a few tears. When the tears were flowing, I talked to the first sergeant on duty, Scotty. I told him that my grandmother was dead and that I needed a three-day pass. My grandmother had been dead for years. Apparently the sergeant thought that my grandmother had just passed away and probably felt sorry for me because he gave me the three-day pass with his sincere condolences. After the second day off post, two military police found me drunk. They tried to arrest me, but I had been trained in judo. I took both of their sticks away from them and threw the clubs on top of a nearby building. My luck did not hold, because along came their sergeant. He asked his men what had happened. When they told him, he looked at me and ordered me to get into the jeep. I told the sergeant that I did not want to get into the jeep. When I saw the sergeant unbuckle his weapon, I told him I had changed my mind and got into the jeep. He took me back to the post, and the provost officer on duty asked me if I had a pass. I held a pass up to where the provost officer could see it and then tore it up in small pieces. You see, I did not want to get my sergeant in trouble, because I considered him a good guy. Then I pretended that I was drunker than what I really was. The provost officer did not like my behavior. He called me a nice guy and banged my head against the jail bars. He said, "So you want to be tough? I am writing you up for everything I can think of."

The delinquency report was four pages in length. The next morning, First Lieutenant Bealer, the company commander, came into his office. He had that four-page delinquency report in front of him. The lieutenant wanted to know why I got drunk and was away from my post. I said, "Sir, I just got in with the wrong crowd, and I needed to get away from them to break the cycle. I can now straighten up and be a good soldier." The commander gave me an article 15, which was a disciplinary action. He told my corporal stripes and put me on fourteen days of hard labor.

While at hard labor, I reported to the orderly room one Sunday morning. The soldier in charge asked me to answer the telephone while he went to eat breakfast. The first telephone call was from First Lieutenant Bealer. When I told him who I was, he said in GI language, "What the hellfire are you doing answering the telephone? You are supposed to be on disciplinary action." I explained to him the circumstances surrounding my actions, and he accepted my reason for being there. The lieutenant wanted me to check the sign-out log to see if a certain three soldiers had signed out. Lieutenant Bealer said, "Make sure these soldiers signed out." I went over to the sign-out log and then went back to the phone and said, "All three soldiers are checked out." The three solders had been killed while driving across Yackima Mountain, and everything had to be in order before the soldiers' insurance would pay their families. The major wanted to make sure that every detail was in order.

Chapter XII

When we got our orders to go to Korea, a lady friend came to see me, and I left post with her. When I returned, my bag with my steel pot on top was sitting out in my company area. I had already gotten my boarding number, so my girlfriend gave me a ride to my ship.

I had been drinking all morning, and when I boarded the ship, I was high as a kite. My helmet was on backwards, and when my company commander and first sergeant called my number, I took the helmet off my head to read my number. I said, "That's me" and staggered aboard ship. My company commander, First Lieutenant Bealer, questioned me about the lady I was with; I told him that she was my sister. My friend had visited me every day while I was on extra duty. First Lieutenant Bealer said, "You know that is not allowed." Then he said, "Harrumph." He ordered my bag searched. In my bag I had packed eight or nine pints of whiskey. I had wrapped each bottle very carefully so that it wouldn't break. There were two decks between my commanding officer, my first sergeant, and me. I yelled, "Be alert; bag coming down." I dropped my bag down those two flights of stairs, and it landed right in front of my platoon sergeant. The sergeant said, "Damn, there couldn't be any whiskey in this bag. The bottles would have broke all to hell if there had been." My bag was not searched and I carried whiskey all the way to Korea.

One dark night at sea, while having a nip with my friend, our first sergeant came around the corner. This sergeant had a nose for booze. He informed us that having booze on board the ship was illegal and that we could end up in the stockade when we landed. I said to the first sergeant, "We have done nothing wrong. We were standing here by this gun and my foot happened to kick a bottle; then I discovered it was a bottle of booze. The seal on the bottle had not yet been broken. My friend and I broke the seal, tasted the booze, and it was good. We have had enough, and someone else can have the rest." I also pointed out that if I were in the stockade it might save my life. My friend and I walked away. Nothing more was said about the booze.

19

When we arrived in Pusan, my whiskey was intact. I took the whiskey out of my bag and hid about half of it in the kitchen truck toolbox. On our fist bivouac, a few miles out of Pusan, Chen, the mess sergeant asked if he could take a bottle of my whiskey over to the officers and non-commissioned officers' meeting. I told him where the stash was and warned him not to tell anybody else. After the meeting, the first sergeant came over to me and asked, "Did you bring that bottle of booze onboard our ship?"

I said, "Sergeant, you know the story. If you want to put me in the stockade, go ahead. There is combat a little way up the road."

Chapter XIII

I saw my first action when the North Koreans kept trying to push the United Nations troops back into the sea at Pusan. Since I was driving a kitchen truck along the front lines, I was allowed to have a fifty-caliber gun on a mount. I took the gun with me every trip I made out to the lines.

The North Koreans were coming out across a rice paddy that was about two miles in length. My battalion, the Second Engineer Battalion, was told to set up a defensive line because the infantry were retreating and the communists were plunging through our lines. While the North Koreans were snaking their way across a nearby rice paddy, they were using us as target practice. I went to my truck, removed the fifty-caliber gun, and set it up behind a nearby sandbag castle. My assistant, a man named Gonzales, and I crouched behind the sandcastle, watching the enemy approach us. Across my head I wore an earphone with a microphone to talk to my commander during the coming skirmish. Suddenly, I heard a voice say into my ear, "There's a sniper behind you." I wheeled around with my fifty-caliber gun and pushed my head against the sandbag castle. I said, "Gonzales, put your head down." I looked through the gun site and saw movement at the base of a nearby tree. I fired one round of bullets, the sniper fell, and his weapon went eight or nine feet in the air. I could not determine whether I had shot him or if someone else had shot him. I yelled to my company commander that the sniper had been hit and that I saw him lose his weapon. During the heat of exchanging fire with the enemy, one of the sniper's bullets grazed the bridge of my nose and hit the sandbag with a thud beside my face. I did not realize what had happened until my assistant, Gonzales, told me what he saw. He was down in the foxhole looking up at me.

Chapter XIV

Our company commander decided to move our defensive position about four miles back. He told me to hold the advancing troops back with my field of fire. He told me to destroy my weapon and move out when the Korean Army got too close. I made up my mind that I was not going to destroy my weapon. I decided to hold out as long as I could. My friend Smitty was my company commander's driver. I asked Smitty to pass the word to my company commander that I had decided to hold on to the gun as long as I could. Smitty told me he would tell him. I asked Smitty to bring back a half-track or tank and park at the bend of the road away from my already-established position. I wanted Smitty and whoever he brought back to be well out of my line of fire. Smitty found a half-track and told the driver where to park it. Smitty explained to the soldiers manning the track what was going on, and they began defensive firing with their quad tract 50 gun. Meanwhile, Smitty came to get me in his jeep. We loaded my weapon into the vehicle and headed back to our line of defense.

We went through a small town, and I spied the message "Kilroy was here," on a bombed-out building's wall. Smitty and I thought we were the first soldiers in this unoccupied town, but the nose and hands on the wall let us know that our soldiers had been in this town before us. We went down what we considered the main street of the little town. The town's bank, which was located on the corner of Main and another street, had been bombed. Korean money was everywhere. Smitty and I stopped, jumped out of the jeep, and picked up some of the Korean money for souvenirs.

We found our lines just outside the little town. To my left there was a cliff with a drop off of about twenty or thirty feet, a dry river bed a little to my right with a bridge, and a ditch running parallel to the riverbed. I reported to my company commander and asked him where he wanted me to set up my weapon. He told me to use my own judgement.

Chapter XV

I climbed a nearby hill and looked around. I could see the main road leading to the little town, the deep ditch, the bridge, and the dry riverbed. I knew this was the best place that I could find, because I would have a firing range of all advancing movement. Gonzales and I set up my fifty-caliber gun, tied a small tree to the barrel for camouflage, and crouched down to wait. We were told to hold our positions at all costs. We knew that we would have to fight to the death if need be.

When I began to fire the fifty-caliber gun, the smoke and the smell of burning oil off the hot gun was so strong that the smoke burned the inside of my nose. It wasn't a hot day, but I could feel the sweat running down my back. My body was hurting because I had stayed in a crouched position so long. The day was fading into night, and a heavy, dense fog began to roll in. I kept firing into the range of fire that I had chosen. I saw at least eight Koreans fall before the light faded.

During a break in my random firing, Gonzales and I heard a noise in front of me. I thought that someone was crawling through the bushes. I eased my head up and spied a woman coming out of the fog carrying a baby on her back. I looked at the baby and noticed that his arm had been almost severed and was hanging to his shoulder by a muscle. I reached out, got her and the baby, and pulled her beside me. I yelled into my microphone to send a medic immediately. When the medics arrived, they wanted to know what they were supposed to do with this woman and baby. I said, "Take them to the field hospital." I did not know if the baby could be saved, but I knew they could stop the bleeding. When I went out after the woman and baby, I knew that I was risking my life. We had been told before going into combat that some Korean women carried grenades and that their intentions were to blow up any United Nations soldier. I knew I was in danger and that I was going against the rules, but I made a judgement call.

Around midnight all hell broke loose. My company commander told me that there was hand-to-hand combat going on with the first squad. I told my company commander that if he would have all the soldiers in hand-to-hand combat take cover, I would fire in the direction of the fighting. I fired several rounds in the fighting area. Later, after the battle, I learned that my best friend was in one of the foxholes that I shot over while shooting at the enemy. I was told that he died from a heart attack. I felt guilty because I thought that I might have caused his death.

To my left, above the cliff, there were four machine guns firing at the enemy. The Koreans were coming around a small hill into their line of fire. The Koreans scattered, trying to get away from the machine gun fire. Some of these men headed toward the cliff. When they ran around it, they found that it was not an escape route. They could not go back, nor could they go forward, so they jumped off the cliff. When they jumped, they fell through thick vegetation, and their hats got tangled in the matted growth. They hung there until they died.

A T-34 Russian tank began firing over my head. His rounds of fire kept hitting the hill behind me. By the time the tank had fired three rounds, I knew I was safe because he didn't have the proper elevation on his weapon to zone in on my position.

All through the night, Gonzales and I stayed on the side of the hill firing into the foggy night. The actual battle lasted for four hours and ten minutes. At daybreak we backed away and rested. I wanted to check out my parameter of fire, but my sergeant said that the area had been checked out. He said they found that one hundred twenty Korean soldiers had been killed in my parameter of fire. I believe they kept me away from the scene because it would have been too traumatic for me to see all that destruction.

I talked to my commander about the tank that had been firing at Gonzales and me. I asked him if I could have a weapon big enough to wipe out a tank. I wanted to get that son of a bitch (my favorite words) before he tried to shoot someone else. He assigned me a 3.5 rocket launcher that would put a big hole in any kind of tank. He also sent two more men with Gonzales and me. When I got to the place where the tank had been, he was gone. He would live a little while longer.

.

Chapter XVI

After resting all day, we got orders to head north. The North Koreans were pushing south across the Naktong River about four miles north of our resting-place. At the Naktong River, my engineer battalion and I built a floating bridge for the Inchon landing. The Inchon landing was a massive buildup of United Nations Forces troops coming ashore to push the Koreans back north. What was left of our division was under the protection of the Ninth Infantry, a regiment of the Indian Head Second Infantry Division.

The North Koreans were on the opposite side of the river waiting for us. When we finished the bridge we were building, they cranked their tanks up and began to cross the floating bridge. We evacuated and the infantry took over, surrounding the North Koreans and their tanks. The North Koreans began to retreat north. My group of engineers followed the retreating soldiers and killed stragglers and snipers along the way. At this moment, MacArthur made the Inchon landing while we pushed the retreating Koreans back across the thirty-eighth parallel. We moved all the way up to just below Seoul in the Inchon area where we bivouacked.

Chapter XVII

November 4, 1950, the company clerk called me into his tent and told me that because of my performance in the last battle, I had been recommended to receive a Silver Star for valor. He indicated it was all on paper. This recommendation came from Lieutenant Shallon and Sergeant Fox. At that moment, before I could get my Silver Star, we got word that the Chinese had entered the war. Everything was in a state of frenzy. All paperwork was destroyed. I was sorry then and later, because I might have been able to trade that medal for a cup of coffee. But all our focus was on the fact that we had two enemies: the Chinese and the North Koreans.

Chapter XVIII

We were at Inchon in November 1950 when we heard rumors that we would be home before Christmas. Little did I know that I wouldn't see my homeland for another thirty-three months or more. We pushed north toward the Chinese border. We met the Chinese about four or five miles south of the Yalu River. The clash of arms was furious. The Chinese pushed several of our fighting infantry and cavalry into an enclosed U-line of fighting. The Chinese had woven their way through wooded areas and had gotten behind us. At the Chosin Reservoir, General Lewis Puller and his marines fought one of the most courageous and tough battles in marine history. The Chinese surrounded them, and they had to fight their way through the Chinese lines.

We were in retreat when we came into a valley. We were told that the enemy surrounded us. Our southern route had been closed off, and the Chinese were on both sides of us. We were the only engineer regiment in the valley. Our group, along with the artillery unit, consisted of approximately three hundred men. We were given orders to take the roadblock to the south and open it up for at least three days so that eleven hundred men could retreat. We were told to help the fighting troops that were pinned down to get back through the lines. When the Chinese figured out what we were doing, they sent a force of soldiers to meet us. We were hit pretty hard, and our escape route was again closed. We were totally surrounded and were pinned down by machine gun fire. There was no place for us to go, so we stayed there all that day until about midnight. Word was passed from man to man down the line: "break out," "break out." With the exception of a few engineers, I was among soldiers who were not in my former group. I was at the most southern part of our defense.

We began to advance toward machine guns. About forty of us broke through the Chinese defense. In the heat of the battle, while advancing toward the machine guns, my feet continued to take me toward the gunners even though my brain was numb. The adrenaline kept pumping in my body as I got close enough to shoot at the machine gunner. He threw a concussion grenade under my feet; in my crouched stance, the blast flipped me up in the air and back into my place. I kept firing as I advanced. A second grenade rolled under my feet, and with the blast I again went into the air, turned completely around, and came down running. Later I discovered that I had shrapnel right below my knee, but I was not hurt that badly. I veered off the gunner's line of fire and kept advancing toward him. Finally, the gunner quit firing, and I knew that I had shot him. For the third time, I saw the elephant.

Chapter XIX

We moved quietly through the moonlit night, always heading south. We came over a hill and saw a small Korean village. I chose a man named Cameron to be my point man. Cameron scouted out the town, and when he came back reported that there were machine guns positioned on both sides of the village. I knew we couldn't go back because the Chinese were behind us. We had to go forward. I snuck up as close to the town as I could get and observed that the town was not occupied with civilians. We moved toward the town, yelling like wild Indians. As we advanced, the Chinese began to come out of the huts, shooting back at us, but we kept charging forward. They dropped like flies. Finally the town was quiet, and then we moved on.

There were only eight of us left when we entered new territory, and we didn't know what to expect. We came to a wide ditch about twelve feet deep. There had to be a bridge to cross. Our point man, Cameron, came back without a report that there was a walk bridge down to the right. Walking along the ditch toward the bridge, we discovered there were Chinese hiding in the ditch. This was the first and last time in my career that I gave the order to kill. I said to my men, "If he has a weapon, kill him." We moved on across the ditch and came upon a small hill. Cameron left us, and when he came back, he told us that there was a small group of villagers huddled with their belongings and animals on top of the next hill. I ordered my men to train their weapons left. I told them that if we were fired up on to return the fire. We passed by the civilians without confrontation. I talked with Cameron and told him that we needed to maneuver into the next valley while the moon was still out. One of the infantrymen asked me why. I told him that I wanted the civilians to see where we were going. Then we would do a right flank to move out of harm's way. I said that the civilians would probably report to the Chinese that we were on the next hill. Artillery and mortars would then be used to tear up the hill and try to kill us. My plan worked and we moved on.

We hid out during the day, and at night we wove our way through Chinese lines heading south. On the last day of November, a group of low flying planes came in, strafed the area, and spotted our group. They were ours! We put our marker out (a large piece of red plastic) to let them know that we were friendly. We ran downhill, and the planes strafed an area around us in case we were to come under fire from the enemy. We got to the road, and ran into a platoon of Chinese soldiers dug into the side of the roadway. They saw us and opened fire over our heads. I told my remaining eight men to keep firing and maybe we could shoot our way out. We were firing; in a fleeting moment, I saw some of the Chinese were still firing over our heads. My gun jammed, and two Chinese soldiers jumped me and twisted the gun out of my hand. In just seconds, I had become a prisoner of war.

Chapter XX

A young Chinese soldier, who I had recognized as an officer because he had one red stripe below his elbow, knew that I was the leader. He began to question me. I realized he was an educated man because he spoke some English. While I was being questioned, I noticed a Chinese solder inching his way behind me with a machine gun. I grabbed the officer who was questioning me and danced with him until he was between the Chinese gunner and me. The officer knew that I was protecting myself. He reached over and slapped the machine gunner across his face.

The Chinese moved us up a hill among their platoon. A group of U.S. planes spotted us; since I was still dragging my marker behind me, I assumed they knew that we were among Chinese troops. Four planes came in toward us, and I told my men to spread the marker, take their hats off, and raise their left hands so the pilots in the planes could see our name tags. We stood straight as the plane came toward us. At that point, when they normally would have fired, the pilots recognized who we were and pulled off. It seemed as if my heart had stopped beating, and then I could feel it beating again. I had played my last card and won.

At that time, I thought that when the planes came in close they snapped our pictures. I found out three years later that I was correct in assuming that our pictures had been taken. My family received word that I was recorded as a prisoner of war instead of missing in action. Harry S. Truman signed the letter to my family. At this point in my story, I would like to thank those Navy pilots for being able to discern that we were friends and not foes. They tried to give us assistance and help us to stand tall in the presence of our captors.

Chapter XXI

It was December 1950 and the first night of captivity. Our Chinese captors marched us down a hill, across a set of tracks, and into a railroad tunnel, where they were hiding out from our planes. When I entered the tunnel and my eyes adjusted to the light, I noticed a few other POWs being guarded by the Chinese. We stayed the rest of the night and all the next day. Our guards fed us rice, and we were glad to get it. We had not eaten in three days. My last can of C rations was a can of chicken that I split with another soldier.

I noticed that some of the Chinese recruits were very young, and it was apparent that they knew very little about their weapons. One young soldier was playing with his gun and suddenly the gun discharged. The bullet ricocheted off the walls of the tunnel. My men thought that that this incident was hilarious. The Chinese colonel got up, went over, and slapped the young man hard with the back of his hand across the recruit's face.

Under the cover of darkness, we started our march north toward the POW camps. While walking the first ten miles, a battle had raged between the United Nations forces and the Chinese. It appeared that the United Nations forces were trying to break the Chinese lines so they could head south. I noticed that there were abandoned vehicles everywhere and dead United Nations soldiers and Chinese soldiers. I saw that for every one United Nations soldier dead, there were twenty to twenty-five dead Chinese. I could see that the United Nations soldiers had used all their fire power, artillery, and tanks.

On our first night of marching, we were crossing a thirty-mile mountain. The Chinese fed us as well as themselves. We ate whole kernel corn that was like hominy that we had back home. However, back home we would boil the corn long enough to get the hull off. We were trying to eat the corn with the hull still on when a fellow prisoner said, "I can't eat this." I said, "I bet the Chinese soldiers have eaten this corn all their lives. Watch how they eat it." We watched the soldiers as they took a spoonful of corn and put it into their mouths, rolled it around until it softened, and eventually the corn was chewed and swallowed. I looked over at my buddy and saw him rolling corn around in his mouth.

We marched north about thirty miles each day, and as we passed through small towns and POW stopovers, we picked up more prisoners. For every mile we walked we lost a man or two. This reminded me of the World War II march from Corrigador.

As we marched, we seemed to be heading toward the farthest point in China. The weather turned cold, and it got down to about thirty degrees below zero at night. The snow was so deep that we had difficulty walking.

When we made camp, our Chinese guards divided our group into officers, enlisted men, and non-commissioned officers. Our Chinese captors did not want the enlisted men influenced by their sergeants or officers.

Chapter XXII

On December 25, 1950, we were crossing a thirty-mile mountain, and at about midnight, our men began to sing "Silent Night" and other Christmas carols. The Chinese guards became very disturbed. A Chinese soldier who knew the English language told the guards that we were worshiping our Gods with our singing. The guards let us continue to sing.

We marched about thirty miles a day in the extreme cold, and our feet, hands, faces, and ears were getting frostbitten. The year 1950 was the coldest winter in recent history. The word was passed down the line to cover our skin that was exposed to the elements with loose clothing. At night when we stopped to rest, we tried to doctor ourselves as best we could. When our men died, they were loaded onto a cart drawn by oxen.

Chapter XXIII

We kept moving north. All along the march were camps that were classified as POW stopovers. At the first stopover, the weather was still cold and the snow was about ten inches deep. I was sent over to Chinese headquarters to talk to an English reporter for the Communist Party newspaper, the *Daily Worker*. In my mind, I set up a resistance to the brainwashing slanted toward Communist propaganda that I knew I was going to get. I decided that I would not listen to this reporter's Communist preaching, and I was successful. I turned him off in my mind.

The reporter asked me what I was doing in Korea and other similar questions. He asked me, "Why are you being the aggressor against peace-loving people?" I stopped him in the middle of his question and declared, "Who are you calling peace-loving people? You North Koreans were the ones who came across the thirty-eighth parallel, and the Chinese have jumped into a damn war that they have no business being in. This is a United Nations forces peacekeeping force that I am fighting for. However, it looks like you, an Englishman, are a traitor to your own country. You are a son of a bitch, and I have nothing else to say to you."

The Englishman sent me back to my hut, and I told my fellow inmates about him and what he was trying to do. I told them what I had said to him. We all knew that the intense interrogations that we were getting were Communist slanted, and we had to somehow guard ourselves against their sly and subtle brainwashing techniques.

Because the weather was bad, our guards stayed close in our camp. We had very little to eat—only millet and rice. We were always cold and miserable. We were allowed to make fires in our huts on a grill called a hibachi.

The huts were about nine feet by nine feet. The floor was made of dirt with tunnels to let the heat warm the room. We slept on the floor, and as the night advanced toward dawn, our beds became harder and harder. All through the night we would cross our legs right over left and then left over right. This would go on all night to relieve the weight of our bodies.

One day while on a wood detail, we passed one of the Chinese kitchens. I looked in the open door and saw a ham hanging from the rafters. I made up my mind that these sons of bitches were not going to starve me to death. If there was food within reach, I was going to get it.

Later I crawled back about fifteen yards and stopped in front of a guard. I bellied around him and down to the kitchen. When I finally entered the kitchen, I saw that the ham was gone, but I saw a big pot of rice. I had on a field jacket with all kinds of pockets. I filled each pocket full of rice. I then bellied my way back through the snow. In our hut, I divided the rice among all the men.

One day I stepped out of my hut onto the ground when I noticed a corporal standing to one side coughing and shivering. Nearby the corporal was a North Korean captain. I went over to the corporal and asked him what was going on. He told me that he had stolen a handful of soybeans out of a huge sack of soybeans. I relieved him of duty and told him to go back to his hut and lie on the warm floor until his congestion had loosened up. Then I went over to the Korean captain, saluted him so he wouldn't lose face, and told him that I would take the corporal's place.

When we marched north again, we marched through small villages, where we picked up more prisoners. Always the civilians would be lined up on the side of the road cheering our captors. These villagers had sold out to Communism. We were the bad guys, and the villagers were glad we were prisoners of war.

Chapter XXIV

We spent several months marching north toward camp 5. While walking into the camp, a prisoner came up to me and said, "I saw you get blown all to hell with a grenade.

I said, "You cannot believe everything that you see, since I am standing right here in front of you."

When I was settled into my quarters, I was assigned latrine detail with a group of POWs. We went into the nearby woods and dug a long ditch. This was our latrine, or toilet in layman's terms. A shovel was nearby, and when a man needed to relieve himself, he would use the ditch and cover the dung with a shovel of dirt.

In the first few days in camp 5, I discovered that the Chinese distributed the *Daily Worker*, a newspaper for the Communist. I had seen this paper before when I worked in an automobile factory in Detroit. Someone at our boarding house left the paper lying around. I read the paper then and thought it was bullshit, and now I still think it is bullshit. I was familiar with Lenin's and Karl Marx's political views because I had researched them extensively.

Our Chinese guards would lay the *Daily Worker* around where we would pick it up and read it. I did not read the paper for war information, because I knew stories and incidents simply were not true. But I read this paper to assist me in thinking what my next interrogation would be.

Because I had called the Englishman, the first man who interrogated me, a traitor, I was marked as a reactionary. I would be pulled away from my group and harassed. They were trying to get information from me.

Since I was a reactionary, the POWs around me singled me out to talk to me. I always tried to be honest with my answers, and these men trusted me. They knew I was not a Communist snitch.

One morning I was outside returning from the river when I met an Irish corporal. He said to me in his Irish brogue, "Good morning, father."

I didn't understand what he said to me and asked, "What did you say?"

He said, "I said good morning, father."

"I am not a priest," I told the corporal.

"But everyone comes to you for advice," he said.

I was amazed that this man thought that I was a priest. Later, when I thought about what had happened, I figured out why I was being interrogated so often.

After awhile, soldiers from other groups sought me out. Since the Chinese observed this, they watched me closely. It was truly an honor to be trusted by my fellow prisoners of war. At all times, I tried to maintain honor and fairness.

Food was always the main issue with all of us. My group wanted someone to be in charge of the food. They wanted someone to oversee the food and divide the food fairly among all the prisoners. I was elected to do this job. It was a great honor for me to know that these men trusted me enough to put me in charge of their food. It was also a tremendous responsibility for me, since having enough food meant the difference between life and death.

For a year, we lived on rice twice a day. The portions measured about half a canteen cup of rice. We were losing men from dysentery, pneumonia, and many other diseases that plagued us. We were literally starving to death at a slow rate.

In my second year as a prisoner of war, a Chinese guard gave our cook rice flour. The cook came to me for help. I told him that I would build a Dutch oven. I asked the guards if I could have fence post bricks, a hammer, a chisel, and a couple of oil drums. I finished the Dutch oven, and it was ready to go.

A Chinese guard came by while I was building the oven. He offered me a pack of cigarettes. I asked, "Do you have a pack of cigarettes for every prisoner in this compound?"

He said, "No."

I said, "Then forget about it. I will not accept anything that can't be equally divided among all the other prisoners."

I talked to the cooks about the oven, and then they wanted to know how they could get the dough to rise since they did not have baking powders. I told them about the British sailors during World War I who ate lime to keep from getting beriberi, and that is why they were called limeys.

The cook asked the guards if they could have lime to put in the bread. The Chinese gave us lime, Chinese cabbage that looked like our lettuce, and soybean oil. Out of the rice flour our cooks made pancakes. For once we had all the food that we could eat.

When spring came, I would go and sit on a hill near our camp. I would choose real tender new grass, pull it up, and take it back to camp to par boil it. I then would pour the first water off and put a few spoonfuls in my rice. I felt that this helped me stay a little healthier.

Our hospital was a makeshift shack where our sick men were taken to die. One day I received word from my friend Chen that he was in the hospital and wanted to see me. Chen, a mess sergeant and a friend, had been in our kitchen truck driver's pool before we left the States. Chen knew he was dying, and he wanted me to tell his family about his life as a prisoner. Chen told me, "You will be a survivor." I assured him that I would talk to his family, but I knew that I had to inform my debriefer after the war. Once a death was proved, the army usually sent a chaplain to talk to the family. But I would try.

One of my soldier friends, Katerio, became sick with beriberi. His legs were swollen, and I was told that if the swelling went up to his throat, he would suffocate. I would make a broth of grass and carry it to him every day, or I would carry him to the cook shack, and I made sure he had half of the broth I made.

I believe that if I had not helped Katerio, he would have died. A few months after I was released from prison, I was stationed at Fort Belvoir, Virginia. I found out that Katerio was at Walter Reid Hospital in Washington, D.C. I went to visit him several times while he was there. His family wrote me a letter thanking me for saving Katerio's life. Although Katerio had to wear thick binocular glasses and he was ill off and on for the rest of his life, he was with his family.

The Chinese continued to war on the physical and mental being in other camps but doing such things as pouring water and human waste on prisoners in holes and leaving them to freeze to death. In our camp they continued their brainwashing techniques by planting seeds of Communism in our minds. I noticed that they revised their tactics every few days.

During the coldest part of the winter, when our men died, they stacked them in cold storage areas. When the weather cleared, they were buried on the side of a nearby hill close to a Korean graveyard. The Korean graveyard was neatly kept, and each grave had about an eighteen-inch cone mound on top of the ground. Our American graveyards lay flat with grass sown over the graves.

Chapter XXV

My friend Cameron, who scouted for me after we broke through the Chinese lines and headed south, was sick and not able to leave his bed. Every morning we had to stand in formation to be counted. One of our guards, whom we named "Comrade Rat Face" because he looked like a rat, went to look for Cameron because he was not in formation. My friend tried to explain to Rat Face that he was too sick to get up. Rat Face kicked Cameron hard and tried to make him move. When I returned to our hut, Cameron told me what Rat Face had done. I told Cameron that I was going to break Rat Face of kicking sick men.

The following morning, I stayed in the hut with Cameron instead of going to formation. I sat down in the shadows so Rat Face couldn't see me when he first came in. Rat Face came into the hut yelling at Cameron. He did not notice me until I spoke to him. I said to Rat Face, "If you kick my friend again, I'm going to kill you right here, you son of a bitch." Rat Face became afraid, turned around, and fled from the hut.

When I went into formation, I found Rat Face surrounded by his Chinese buddies. Thinking that the guards would protect him from me, he came over and slapped me on the shoulder. I know that he had intended to slap my face, but somehow missed. In an instant, I grabbed hold of Rat Face and threw his ass down a ten-foot embankment.

I was told to go see the commander of our camp, a colonel in rank. He said to me, "I have heard my soldier's story of how this incident came about, and now I want to hear yours." I told the colonel what had happened that morning. I related to him how Rat Face had kicked my friend Cameron and what I told him I would do if he ever kicked my buddy again. The colonel understood what I told him. He walked over to Rat Face and slapped him across his face. The colonel told me that this would never happen again. He did not use this incident to try to sway me toward Communism. My anti-Communist resolve stayed intact.

My Chinese captors began to interrogate me more often. One day my interrogator said to me, "You lie. I shoot you." He put his pistol to my head, ready to shoot. He pushed the gun hard into the skin between my eyes. I did not let him intimidate me. I pushed my head into the gun as hard as I could, looked straight into his eyes, and said, "Shoot me, you son of a bitch. There are sixteen-hundred graves over the on the side of the hill, and one more won't make any difference." He pulled his gun away, and I breathed a sigh of relief. I had played my last card and won.

Later, when talking to my friend Acres, I asked him what was wrong. He was shaking so hard that his teeth were chattering. He told me a Chinese interrogator had put a gun to his head and threatened to shoot him. He said that he wished he had a cyanide tablet to take because he didn't think he could go through with that torture again. I related to him that everybody was afraid under those kinds of circumstances.

There was going to be one prisoner taken as a token exchange prisoner from our camp. While on detail one day, we walked up a trail between two mountains. There were caves in both sides of these mountains. Just inside the caves were food supplies, arms, and explosives. When I returned to camp, I secretly drew a rough map of the positions of the caves. I sought out the prisoner who was going to be released and asked him to memorize the map and inform his debriefer of its contents. He told me he would do that. In about three weeks, several planes came over our camp and dropped bombs on the cave sites. Everything was destroyed. All the POWs were jumping up and down rooting for our planes. The Chinese never guessed my secret. They thought it was coincidence.

On a sunny cold spring day, my friend Katerio and I were sitting outside a hut. We were leaning back against the mud wall because the wall was warm. A Chinese soldier came down through the camp carrying a five-millimeter machine pistol. He was yelling, "Lattrelle! Lattrelle!"

Katerio said, "He's calling your name."

I said to Katerio, "That son of a bitch is carrying a machine pistol, and I'm not listening to him. Besides, he's saying my name wrong."

The guard went back to his headquarters and got an English-speaking interpreter. The interpreter said to me, "Lattrelle, why you no answer this man? You have to go downtown for interrogation."

I said, "I no answer this man because the son of a bitch was not calling my name. I was not going to walk up to a man carrying a machine pistol."

The guard then marched me to the Chinese headquarters with his machine pistol pointed into my back.

I was taken to a small room. An English-speaking interpreter and a Chinese colonel came into the room. The interpreter told me that the colonel had just come over from China and wanted to interrogate a prisoner. He told me that the colonel did not speak English and that I would have to wait on him to interpret the colonel's Chinese into English and vice versa. I said to the interpreter, "Tell that son of a bitch that all I have for him is my name, rank, and serial number." When the old colonel's face turned red, I knew that he understood what I had just said. The colonel accepted that I had found him out, and he did not lose his temper.

The old colonel began to interrogate me. He asked me one of their favorite questions: "Who do you think will be the victorious force in this war?" I said to the colonel honestly, "There will be no victorious forces in this war. It will be settled across the table by negotiations. You stupid ass people listen to Mao Zedong. I do not know how he figures that he can win this war by springing an army on the United Nations forces. He has to be the most stupid son of a bitch I know."

The old colonel got up and left the room. A prison guard was left standing by the door. My mind went crazy. I knew once again that I had played my last card.

Before I had left Katerio, I told him if he heard a machine gun fire, he could say goodbye to John. I thought that at some point they would decide not to put up with me anymore.

I was left in that small room for about an hour. When I returned to my hut, Katerio was still sitting against the hut wall. Katerio asked, "What did you tell those sons of bitches up there?

I said, "Katerio, I will not tell you what they said until you tell me what went on here."

Katerio related, "They came down here while you were gone and searched every nook and cranny in this hut. They searched everywhere they thought a radio could be hidden, and then they searched every hut in camp."

I told Katerio what I had told the colonel and, without knowing the real truth, had hit the nail right on the head. I said to Katerio, "In about a month we will be told what is happening in this war."

In about three weeks, the Chinese told us that there would be a prisoner exchange at Panmunjom.

Chapter XXVI

On July 27, 1953, the armistice was signed; after several days, our captors started packing us up for the long journey south. The Chinese put us in trucks until we got to the railroad, and then we traveled by train in boxcars over mile-high bridges and rough terrain to reach our destination. The Japanese built the bridges at the time they occupied Korea.

On our arrival, we were put in a holding place. Then they started exchanging the prisoners. The exchange rate was twenty to twenty-five Chinese to one United Nations prisoner. With each exchange, the prisoners crossed the Freedom Bridge. Eventually there were one hundred twenty eight men left, and then we learned that we were being held hostage.

An international advisor was brought in, and he told us that we were being held hostage and that the exchange had been over for a couple of days. The advisor said, "Your own government should be so proud of you people. You were the reactionaries and the ones who resisted the Chinese."

The Chinese POWs crossed the Freedom Bridge in trucks. They were brought by our holding place and driven around a nearby hill. Then we could hear machine gun fire. We didn't know what was going on at first, but later we thought that their men were killing the Chinese.

A couple more days passed, and the rest of us were allowed to cross the Freedom Bridge in Panmunjom.

We were free! We were free!

Chapter XXVII

Our units had been set up and everything was ready for us: food, hot showers, and brand new uniforms.

We were fed and clothed, General Maxwell Taylor, who was in charge of the Far East, met us and shook our hands. Later he made a short speech hailing us as heroes.

We were then put into helicopters and flown to the port of Inchon to board a ship for home. Once on board the ship, my first encounter with a debriefer was with an officer who had no insignia on his uniform. I could tell from the holes in his uniform that he was probably a captain. "Congratulations, Master Sergeant John Luttrell. I congratulate you twice because it is your birthday and the first day of your freedom," the Captain said. The date was September 6, 1953.

The captain then began to question me. He wanted to know if what I had seen as a prisoner of war would be useful for the United Nations forces. Then he asked, "Do you think you have been brainwashed?"

I said to him, "You have used a term that I do not understand." The mental picture that popped into my brain was reaching up, taking my brain out of my head, and washing it with my hands. The word was introduced during the Korean War, and this was the first time I had heard it. When the officer heard what I thought was brainwashing, he laughed. I told him that I did not believe that I had been brainwashed. I told him that I had shut out their propaganda and that I had fought it all the way, but that I had seen a lot of honor lost as a group in the POW camp. I told him that I did not feel some of the soldiers helped their fellow inmates like they should.

I informed him that I volunteered for the United States Army and for missions on the battlefield. I told the captain that we had buried sixteen hundred soldiers at Pyoktong Camp Five due to starvation and lack of medical treatment. I said many soldiers died of dysentery, pneumonia, and beriberi. I informed him that we lost a lot of fellow inmates because we did not help each other. As a result, our honor was lost and our hope was gone.

I told him the location of the graveyard by pointing it out on the map that he handed me. I also told him what I had observed on our way south. There were bomb holes along the railroad tracks and a lot of other damage.

The captain asked me if I had any suggestions based on my experiences as a POW. I told my debriefer that this was the time I had been waiting for and that I'd thought about this while I was a prisoner of war. I said to him that we need something that could be taught in our information hour. I told him that we needed to understand world politics. I explained that a soldier needed to be well trained in all information areas. I continued to inform him that I had been cross-trained by the navy and army and that I had researched politics. I also stated that I had learned many things just by asking questions—mainly from the troops of the Forty First Division in World War II. All this information helped me to survive better mentally because I was sure of what I was doing.

I told my debriefer that I would like to see a code of conduct to assist prisoners if they were being interrogated or punished. He asked me to explain to him what I meant. I suggested that it should be along the same line as the Boy Scout code of honor. He took notes and told me that he would see that this information would be passed along to a higher authority.

As we came into the port of San Francisco, my heart was singing. I wanted to jump up and down. I wanted to run to the gate, down the gangplank, and kiss the ground. I was home! I was home!

While disembarking, I saw Commander Harry Collins watching GIs as they stepped off the ship onto good old American soil (or concrete). Commander Collins, better known as Hollywood Harry because he always wore dark gray sunglasses, commanded the Second Infantry Division. My regiment, the Second Engineer Battalion, was part of Commander Collins's division. When Commander Collins saw me step off the gangplank, he noticed the Indian patch insignia on my shoulder. He cam over, shook my hand, and said a few words to me. I said, "Sir, I recognize you, but I cannot talk to you because I am still being debriefed." Commander Collins was not in uniform; instead, he wore a civilian suit. He understood and stepped away. There was a statement that all soldiers knew and were supposed to abide by: "Loose lips sink ships." Commander Collins's division had been almost annihilated. Only a few men survived. It was rumored later that Commander Collins was relieved of his command because his bad judgement had gotten his men killed.

Chapter XXVIII

I was assigned to Fort Belvoir, Virginia. People from the Pentagon called me, and I went up there three times to advise them on the POW's Code of Conduct. Also they wanted my advice on a movie that had just been made on POW camps. I thought the movie was authentic and appropriate.

Many times government officials from the Pentagon questioned me regarding men in my POW camp who might have betrayed their country. There had been twenty-one people who defected to China, where they found jobs and places to live. They must have felt that Communism was the best thing for them.

My interrogators kept questioning me. I told these men that if a man is starving to death, any small thing—such as a bowl of sugar, and extra bowl of rice, or even a pack of cigarettes—might open that man's mouth.

Even after I had given them my impression of a man's breaking point, they kept coming back wanting names from me who might be traitors. I told them that I would not create a situation for any POW or for myself. I did not know a prisoner who brought harm upon another prisoner, even though all together they did not hold their honor. I told the interrogators that a code of honor was needed and should be taught to officers and enlisted men.

Before I left Fort Belvoir, a young lieutenant came on post and taught the code of conduct for POWs. This code was published in 1953 and was issued to all the personnel in all branches of the military at least once a month. Now it is fifty years later, and I am writing my memoirs. I feel that the code of conduct is a big part of my story because I had a hand in creating it. It was my suggestion.

I saw the elephant three times in the service to my country. For thirty-three months, death was my constant companion. I saw my friends die from disease caused by slow starvation. I saw my body become thin and frail. I survived because I was determined to eat if my captors ate. I looked death in the eye many times but made the right choices. I meant to survive, and the POWs around me could see that. My friend Chen knew that I would live to talk to his family about him. I tried to look beyond myself and help my buddies when I could. I tried to stay sane and turn my mind off when my captors tried to brainwash me with their Communist propaganda. It was sheer determination, hatred for my captors, and the grace of God that got me through. After my imprisonment by the Chinese, I let it be known to my superiors that our American Armed forces needed a code of conduct. I helped to bring that about and am grateful that I had a hand in it. During the last fifty years, I have carried these memories around with me every waking hour. Now I give these memories to my children and my country.

Code of Conduct

For Members of the Armed Forces of the United States

1. I am an American fighting man. I serve in the forces that guard my country and our way of life. I am prepared to give up my life in their defense.

2. I will never surrender of my own free will. If in command I will never surrender my men while they still have means to resist.

3. If I am captured, I will continue to resist by all means available. I will make every effort to escape and aid others to escape. I will accept neither parole nor special favors from the enemy.

4. If I become a prisoner of war, I will keep faith with my fellow prisoners. I will give no information or take part in any action that might be harmful to my comrades. If I am a senior, I will take command. If not, I will obey the lawful orders of those appointed over me and will back them up in every way.

5. When questioned, should I become a prisoner of war, I am required to give name, rank, serial number, and date of birth. I will evade answering further questions to the utmost of my ability. I will make no oral or written statements disloyal to my country and its allies or harmful to their cause.

6. I will never forget that I am an American fighting man, responsible for actions, and dedicated to the principles that made my country free. I will trust in my God and in the United States of America.

C2558493

Enlisted in the RA as Pvt by me this 7 day of
December 1948.
EDWARD B. JORDAN, Capt Inf
2318th ASU

Series C

Honorable Discharge

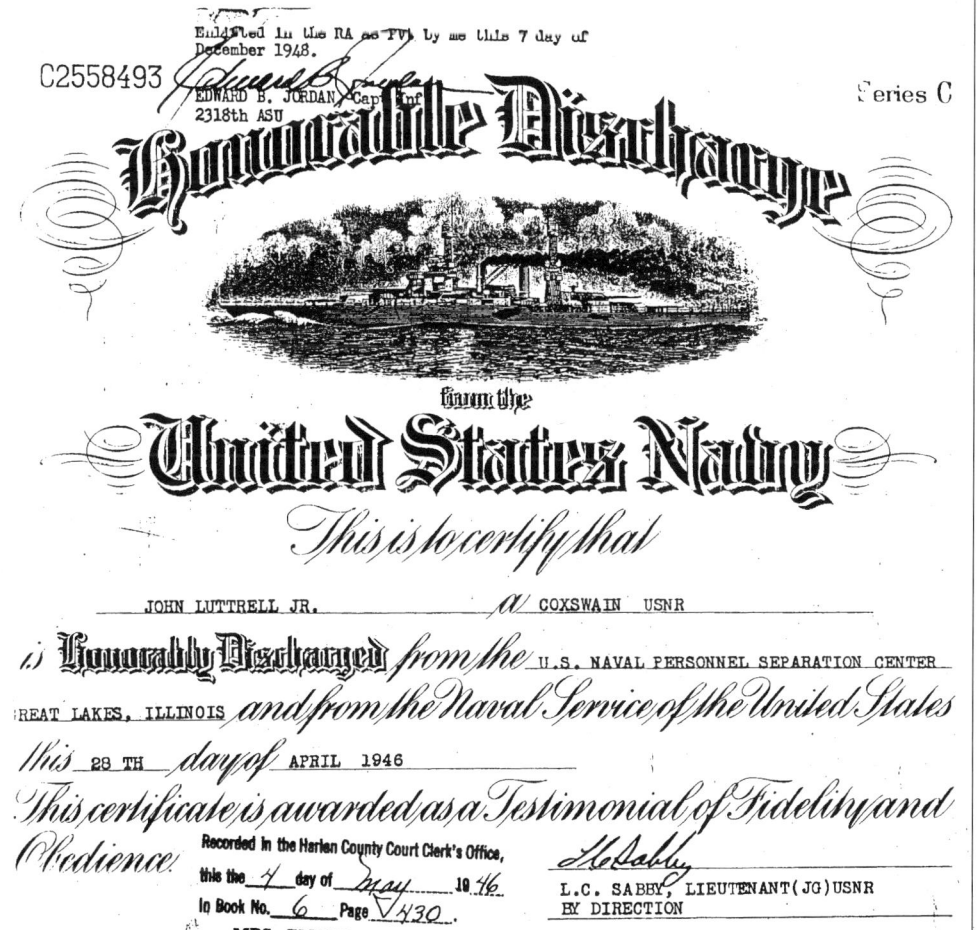

from the

United States Navy

This is to certify that

JOHN LUTTRELL JR.   a COXSWAIN USNR

is **Honorably Discharged** *from the* U.S. NAVAL PERSONNEL SEPARATION CENTER

GREAT LAKES, ILLINOIS *and from the Naval Service of the United States*

this 28 TH *day of* APRIL 1946

This certificate is awarded as a Testimonial of Fidelity and Obedience.

Recorded in the Harlan County Court Clerk's Office,
this the 4 day of May 19 46
In Book No. 6 Page 430.
MRS. ELMON MIDDLETON,
Harlan County Clerk.

L.C. SABBY, LIEUTENANT(JG)USNR
BY DIRECTION

660 (REVISED AUGUST 1945)